atomic reactors

First Published in 1973 by
Macdonald and Company
(Publishers) Limited
St. Giles House
49-50 Poland Street
London W1

Chief Editor:
Ruth Thomson B.A.
Illustrator:
Peter North/The Garden Studio

ISBN 0 356 04616 8
MFL 63

Made and printed in Great Britain
by A. Wheaton & Company
Exeter Devon

MACDONALD FIRST LIBRARY

Fuel and Energy

Macdonald Educational
49-50 Poland Street
London W1

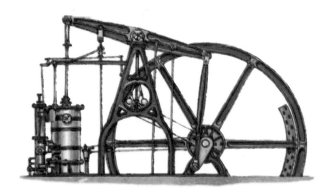

The sun is man's most
important source
of energy.

It provides the light
and heat which help
plants and animals
to live and grow.
Changes in heat make
wind and rain.

The sun warms people and ripens their crops.
At first, man used only his own strength
to till the soil and gather the crops.

Then he tamed animals and harnessed
their strength.

He learned to burn wood to warm himself.
The heat was used for cooking food
and baking pottery.

Men found ways of making work easier.
If many people worked together,
they could pull a very heavy object.
Rollers beneath it helped it slide.
Levers helped to push it along.

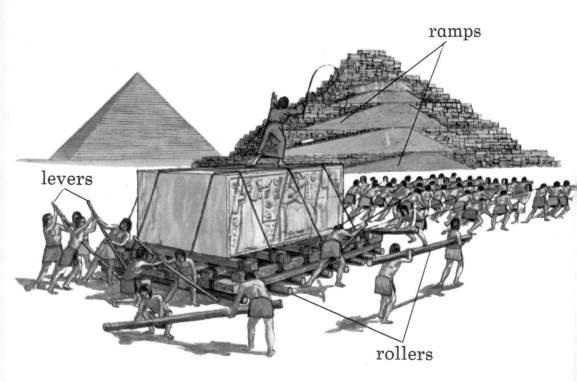

pulley

windlass

anchor

rudder

oar

Sailors used many simple machines.
The oars were levers that pulled the ship along.
The anchor was raised by a windlass.
The sails were raised and set by pulleys,
which made it easier to pull the ropes.

There is natural power on earth
which can be harnessed and used.
The force of flowing water can power
certain kinds of machines.

This is a waterwheel.
Water pours over the wheel and turns it.
The power it produced worked the bellows
and hammer for the blacksmith.

Another kind of natural power used by man is the force of the wind.

This is a windmill. The wind turns its sails. The sails turn cogwheels. One of the cogwheels turns a grindstone. The grindstone grinds corn into flour.

The small sails, called fantails, keep the big sails facing the wind.

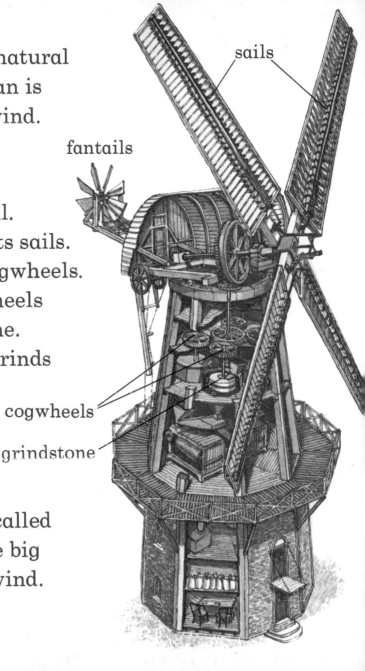

sails

fantails

cogwheels

grindstone

Fuels are substances that produce heat
when they are burned.
The heat is energy that can be used
to power machines.
Coal is a fuel that has been made from trees
that died millions of years ago.

The trees sank into mud.
Over millions of years,
the weight of rocks that
covered the trees
pressed them into coal.

tiny sea creatures

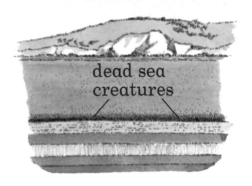
dead sea creatures

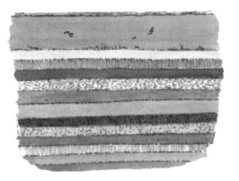

Oil is another fuel.
It is probably made from
tiny dead sea creatures.
When they died, they
sank to the sea bed.
Layers of mud and rock
covered them.
The heavy weight of
folds of rock turned the
creatures into oil.
The folds in the
layers of rock trapped
the oil deep in the earth.

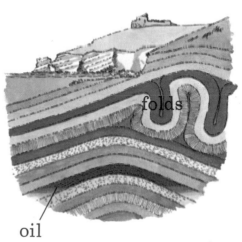
folds

oil

9

Coal lies in layers,
called seams, under
the ground.
Some coal is found near
the surface, but most
coal is deep underground,
or under the sea.

an old coal mine
or 'bell pit'

Modern mines have deep shafts, that reach
down to the coal seams.
Miners dig along the seams, cutting the coal
as they go.

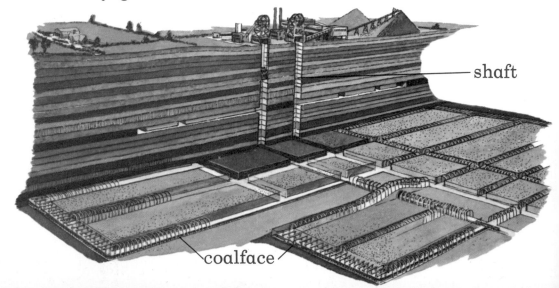

shaft

coalface

pit props

coal carried away
to surface

cutter

Digging for coal is dirty and dangerous.
In most mines today, machines cut the coal.
The coal is carried away on a conveyor belt
from the seam to the shaft.
Lifts carry the coal to the surface.
Pit-props hold up the roof
once the coal has been dug out.

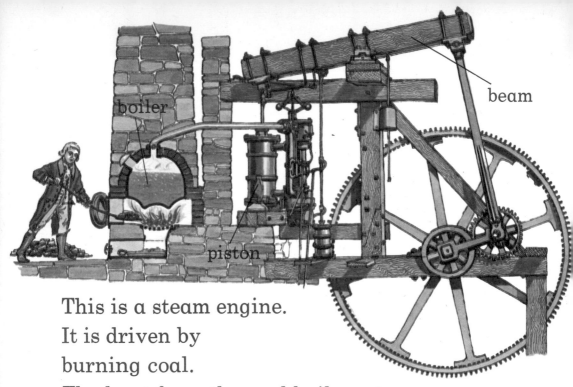

This is a steam engine.
It is driven by
burning coal.
The heat from the coal boils water
to make steam.
The steam pushes a piston, which rocks
the beam at the top, and this turns the wheel.
Steam engines produce more power than men
or animals.
They were used in coal mines to pump out
water and to lift the coal.

Steam engines also powered ships, trains
and factory and farm machinery.
They helped men to travel more quickly
and safely all over the world.
They also powered the machines that made
the ships, trains and factory machines.

Two hundred years ago
this man heated coal in
a kettle without air.
Gas came out.
The coal gas burned.

Many towns built factories to make coal gas.
Gas was used to light homes and streets.
Now gasworks make gas for heating
and cooking.

14

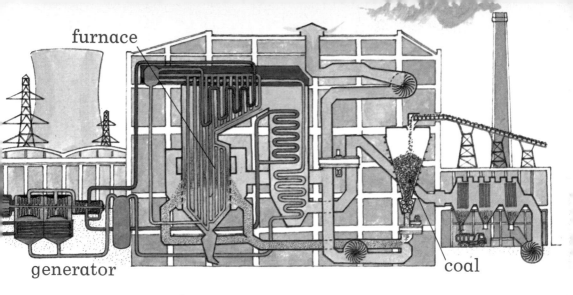

furnace

generator

coal

Coal can be used to make electricity.
Electricity is made in a power station.
In the power station, coal is burned in a furnace.
It heats water to make steam, to drive a turbine.
The turbine spins a dynamo.
The dynamo makes the electricity.

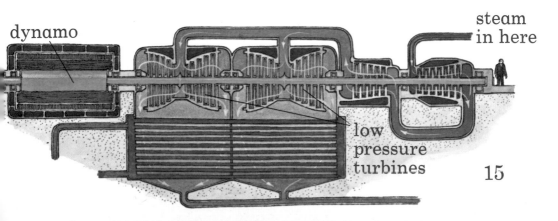

dynamo

steam
in here

low
pressure
turbines

15

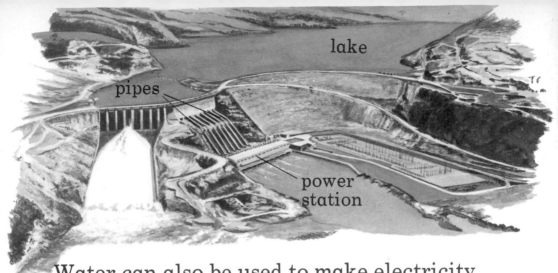

lake

pipes

power
station

Water can also be used to make electricity.
A river is blocked by a high dam
to make a deep lake.
Water behind the dam
runs down steep pipes
to a water turbine.
The water turns the
blades of the turbine.
As the turbine spins,
it turns a dynamo.
The dynamo makes
the electricity.

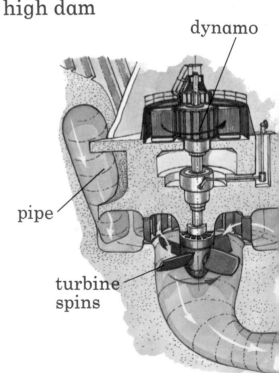

dynamo

pipe

turbine
spins

All kinds of fuel are used in the home.
Coal or coke, gas, oil and electricity
can be used for heating and cooking.
Electricity powers lights
and most household machines.
Life without these fuels would be
much less comfortable.

Oil is found in folds of rock deep in the earth. Men, called geologists, look for these folds. They set off vibrations in the earth with a charge of explosives. Sound waves bounce off the rocks below.

Seismographs measure the time it takes each wave to bounce back to the surface. Each wave is recorded.

fold

oil?

Together they make up a picture of the folds. This picture shows the fold which might hold oil.

Oil is not found in every fold, or anticline.
Holes are drilled to see if oil is there.
It may take a year to drill a hole, and oil
is found in only one out of eight holes.
Anticlines are often
found in out of
the way places.
Tests have been made
in jungles and deserts.
This drill found oil
in Alaska.

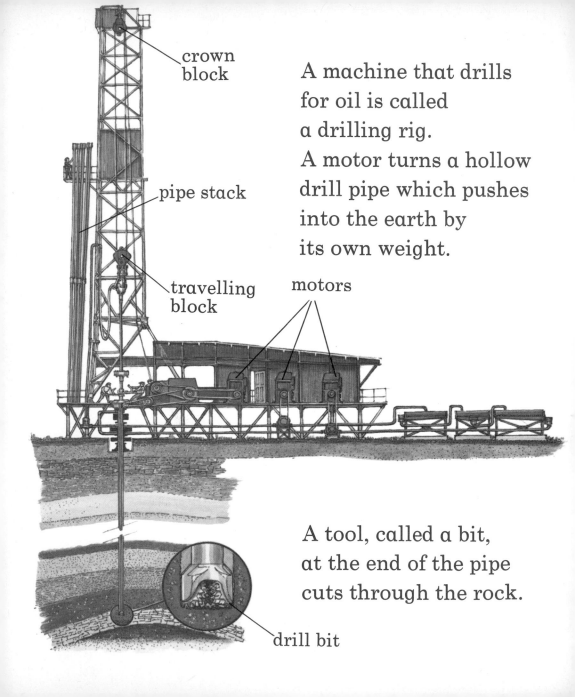

crown
block

pipe stack

travelling
block

motors

drill bit

A machine that drills
for oil is called
a drilling rig.
A motor turns a hollow
drill pipe which pushes
into the earth by
its own weight.

A tool, called a bit,
at the end of the pipe
cuts through the rock.

The top of the pipe hangs from a pulley
at the top of the rig.
As the drill bit bores deep into the ground
more pipe is added at the top.
This is the view down
the inside of the rig.
Men are adding a new
pipe from the stack.

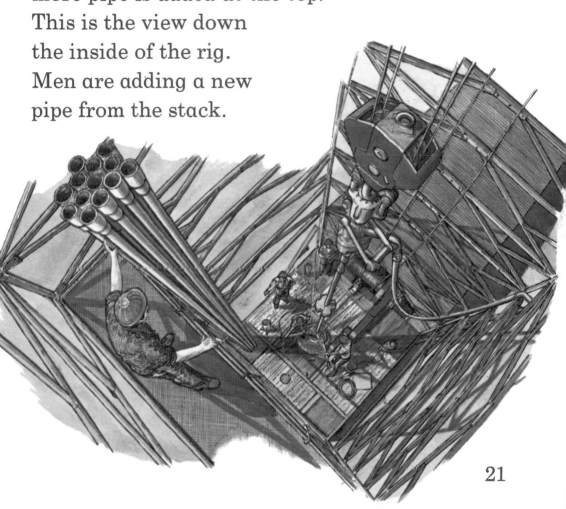

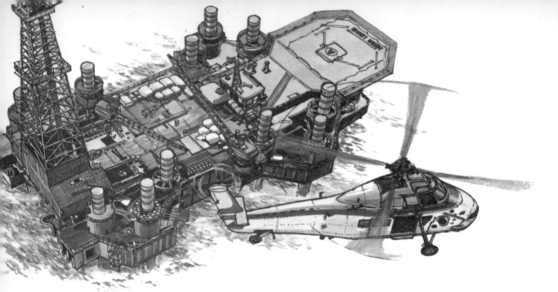

There is gas under the ground as well as oil.
Sometimes oil and gas are found under the sea.
Men drill for them from an offshore drilling rig.
Men live and work on these man-made islands.

When the drill finds oil
or gas, a valve is fitted
to the well.
Then the gas or oil can
be produced safely.
Divers fix pipes to carry
the oil or gas to land.

Oil and gas are often
found in countries that
do not need them all.
They are sold to
countries that do not
have enough fuel.
Ships, called tankers,
carry them across
the sea.
Pipes on land carry
oil and gas to the ports
where tankers load
and unload.

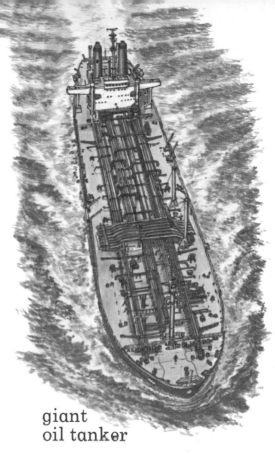

giant
oil tanker

23

Oil comes out of the
ground as a liquid
called crude oil.

Crude oil cannot be
used as it is.
It is taken to an oil
refinery.

There, the crude oil is
broken down into
useful fuels like petrol,
heating and
lubricating oils
and liquid gas.
This is called refining.

Oil is a widely used fuel.
Cars work on petrol.
Jet planes work on pure paraffin.
Lorries, trains and ships use diesel oil.
Buildings can be heated with oil, and some
power stations make electricity with oil.
All machines need oil to run smoothly.
Every machine in this picture
needs oil to make it work.

waterwheel   windmill   water turbine

All these machines are types of engines.
The water wheel, windmill and turbine
use the power of the wind or water.

The engines below use steam to drive them.

early steam engine   steam turbine

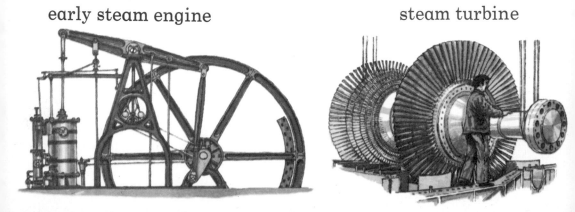

car's petrol engine

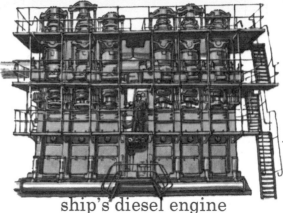
ship's diesel engine

These engines burn fuel inside themselves.
They are called internal combustion engines.
They all burn fuel made from crude oil.
Petrol, diesel oil and paraffin burn more
quickly than coal, and produce more power.

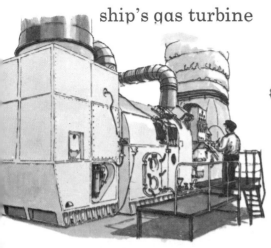
ship's gas turbine

aeroplane's
fan jet

A different kind of
engine is needed to
travel in space.
It is called a rocket.
Special fuel, called
rocket fuel, is used.
It burns very quickly
and pushes the rocket
very fast.
Men have travelled
to the moon and back
in this rocket.

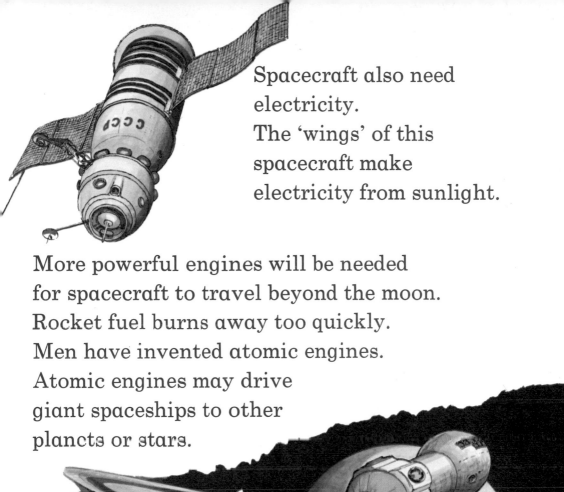

Spacecraft also need
electricity.
The 'wings' of this
spacecraft make
electricity from sunlight.

More powerful engines will be needed
for spacecraft to travel beyond the moon.
Rocket fuel burns away too quickly.
Men have invented atomic engines.
Atomic engines may drive
giant spaceships to other
planets or stars.

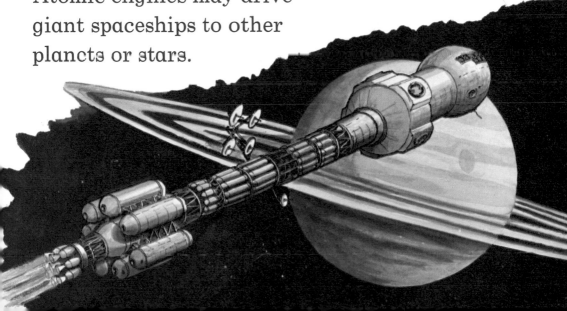

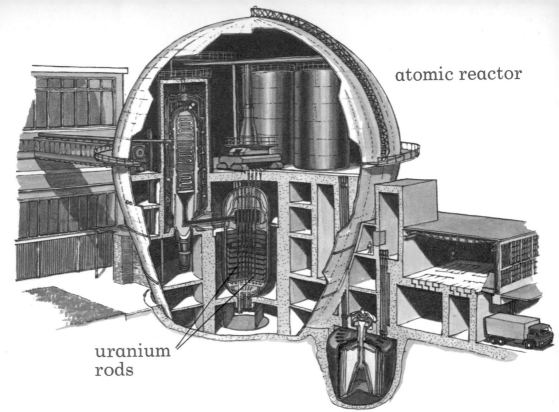

atomic reactor

uranium
rods

All our natural fuels like coal, gas and oil
are slowly being used up.
Men are trying to find new kinds of fuel.
This is an atomic reactor
in a new power station.
It produces heat by splitting atoms.
The heat is used for making electricity.

Even more heat is produced when atoms join
together, or fuse.
The sun's heat is made by fusion.
This machine can hold heat as hot as the sun
without melting.
The heat will fuse atoms.
The heat from the atoms will be used
to make electricity.
We will then be producing heat in the same way
as the sun does, in our power stations on earth.

plasme field
generator

Index

MACDONALD FIRST LIBRARY

1 Prehistoric Animals
2 The Airline Pilot
3 Into Space
4 Knights and Castles
5 The Postman
6 Insects That Live Together
7 By the Sea
8 How Flowers Live
9 Water
10 Number
11 Shape
12 Sounds and Music
13 Cats
14 Frogs and Toads
15 Mushrooms and Toadstools
16 The Policeman
17 Under the Sea
18 Ships of Long Ago
19 Air
20 Cold Lands
21 Spiders
22 Pirates and Buccaneers
23 Size
24 Fire
25 Weather
26 Deserts
27 Skyscrapers
28 Monkeys and Apes
29 Trains and Railways
30 Trees and Wood
31 Cowboys
32 Time and Clocks
33 Light and Colour
34 Birds and Migration
35 The Universe

36 Farms and Farmers
37 Rocks and Mining
38 Rivers and River Life
39 Snakes and Lizards
40 Roads and Motorways
41 Ports and Harbours
42 Bridges and Tunnels
43 Towns and Cities
44 Horses and Ponies
45 Aeroplanes and Balloons
46 The Story of Cars
47 Mountains
48 Electricity
49 Television
50 Photography
51 The Jungle
52 The Dog Family
53 Gypsies and Nomads
54 Ballet and Dance
55 Paper and Printing
56 Food and Drink
57 Cloth and Weaving
58 Lakes and Dams
59 Building
60 Butterflies and Moths
61 Vanishing Animals
62 Animals that Burrow
63 Fuel and Energy
64 Animals with Shells
65 The Theatre
66 Health and Disease
67 Pollution
68 The Cinema
69 Signals and Messages
70 Fishing

oil drilling rig